The Mass for Children

P9-DCP-268

By REV. JUDE WINKLER, OFM, Conv.

Imprimi Potest: Daniel Pietrzak, OFM Conv., Minister Provincial of St. Anthony of Padua Province (USA)
Nihil Obstat: James T. O'Connor, S.T.D., Censor Librorum
Imprimatur: Patrick J. Sheridan, Vicar General, Archdiocese of New York

The Nihil Obstat and Imprimatur are official declarations that a book or pamphlet is free of doctrinal or moral error. No implication is contained therein that those who have granted the Nihil Obstat and Imprimatur agree with the contents, opinions or statements expressed.

© 1990 by CATHOLIC BOOK PUBLISHING CORP., New Jersey

Printed in Hong Kong   ISBN 978-0-89942-489-7

THE MASS

A GIFT FROM JESUS

JESUS loved his apostles so much that he promised them he would never leave them alone. Because he was going to ascend to sit on the right hand of God the Father, he wanted to leave the apostles and us a sign that he would always be with us.

And so, on the night before he died on the cross, Jesus gathered his apostles together for a very special meal. The meal was special for two reasons.

The first reason was that he was celebrating a Passover meal with them. Passover was a feast that the Jews celebrated every year to remember how the Lord had led Israel out of Egypt and how he had freed them from their slavery.

The second reason why this meal was so special was that Jesus was changing it. During the meal he took the bread and told the apostles that it was now his body. He took a cup of wine and told them that it was now his blood. He then told His apostles to continue to do what he was doing in this meal.

This is why we celebrate the Mass. We want to continue to do what Jesus told us to do. This is how we will know that he is always with us until the day he comes back in all his glory.

English translations © 1969 International Committee on English in the Liturgy, Inc.
Other texts and illustrations © 1990 by Catholic Book Publishing Corp., N.Y.

INTRODUCTORY RITES

ENTRANCE SONG — As the priest and ministers go to the altar, the people sing the Entrance Song which begins our celebration of the Mass.

SIGN OF THE CROSS

We Call upon the Holy Trinity

We begin our Mass as we begin any prayer, with the sign of the cross. We are calling upon God to be with us as we pray to Him.

Priest: In the name of the Father, and of the Son, and of the Holy Spirit.

People: Amen.

GREETING

We Are Welcomed in God's Name

The priest then greets us and welcomes us to church. He is speaking not only in his own name, but also in God's name. He uses one of these forms:

A

Priest: The grace of our Lord Jesus Christ and the love of God and the fellowship of the Holy Spirit be with you all.

People: And also with you.

B

Priest: The grace and peace of God our Father and the Lord Jesus Christ be with you.

People: And also with you.

C

Priest: The Lord be with you.

People: And also with you.

4

PENITENTIAL RITE

We Express Sorrow for Our Sins

The priest now invites us to think of our sins and to tell God that we are sorry for them. We want to apologize for having been selfish and for having sinned so that we can listen to God's word and receive His body and blood with a pure heart.

To show our sorrow, we can say:

I confess to almighty God,
 and to you, my brothers and sisters,
that I have sinned through my own fault

We strike our own breasts:

in my thoughts and in my words,
in what I have done,
and in what I have failed to do;
and I ask blessed Mary, ever virgin,
all the angels and saints,
and you, my brothers and sisters,
to pray for me to the Lord our God.

The priest says a short prayer asking for God's mercy.

KYRIE

We Ask Jesus for Mercy

Priest: Lord, have mercy. **People: Lord have mercy.**

Priest: Christ have mercy. **People: Christ have mercy.**

Priest: Lord have mercy. **People: Lord have mercy.**

Sometimes, instead of saying these prayers, the priest asks for God's mercy by calling upon God three times. He finishes his prayer with "Lord, have mercy; Christ, have mercy; Lord, have mercy." We repeat those last words each time he says them.

GLORIA
We Praise God

Now we are so happy God has promised us his forgiveness that we have to celebrate. We do this by saying or singing the song that the angels sang so long ago when they celebrated the birth of Jesus in Bethlehem.

Glory to God in the highest.
and peace to his people on earth.
Lord God, heavenly King,
almighty God and Father,
  we worship you, we give you thanks,
  we praise you for your glory.
Lord Jesus Christ, only Son of the Father,
Lord God, Lamb of God,
you take away the sin of the world:
  have mercy on us;
you are seated at the right hand of the Father:
  receive our prayer.
For you alone are the Holy One,
you alone are the Lord,
you alone are the Most High,
  Jesus Christ,
  with the Holy Spirit,
  in the glory of God the Father. Amen.

OPENING PRAYER
We Join in Prayer Together

This is followed by the Opening Prayer. There are different prayers for each day of the year. In this prayer, the priest asks God to be with us in a very special way as we open our hearts to him.

Priest: For ever and ever.

People: Amen.

OPENING PRAYER — *The priest prays in the name of all who are present. He asks the Lord to guide our thoughts, our prayers, and our love.*

7

LITURGY OF THE WORD

READINGS — *In this part of Mass, we hear the Word of God. Readings taken from the Bible are proclaimed to the people of God. These readings come from both the Old Testament and the New Testament. They speak of God's love for us throughout history and especially of God's love shown to us in Jesus.*

FIRST READING

God Speaks to Us through the Prophets

We sit and listen to the Word of God as it was spoken in the Old Testament, especially through his prophets. The reader takes their place in speaking to us.

At the end of the reading:

Reader: The Word of the Lord.

People: Thanks be to God.

RESPONSORIAL PSALM

We Respond to God's Word

The people repeat the response said by the reader or sung by the cantor.

SECOND READING

God Speaks to Us through the Apostles

We now listen to readings taken from the letters of Paul and the other apostles.

At the end of the reading:

Reader: The Word of the Lord.

People: Thanks be to God.

ALLELUIA VERSE STAND

We Praise Jesus Who Comes to Speak to Us

Jesus will speak to us in the gospel. We rise now out of respect and prepare for his message with the alleluia verse.

GOSPEL — *The priest or deacon reads the gospel in the name of Jesus, and Jesus himself becomes present among us through his word.*

GOSPEL

God Speaks to Us through Christ

The priest or deacon greets us in the name of Jesus.

Deacon (or priest): **The Lord be with you.**
People: And also with you.

Deacon (or priest):
A reading from the holy gospel according to N.
People: Glory to you, Lord.

We listen to the priest or deacon read the Gospel.

At the end of the Gospel:

Deacon (or priest): **The Gospel of the Lord.**
People: Praise to you, Lord Jesus Christ.

HOMILY

God Speaks to Us through the Priest

These readings are God's message to us, but sometimes they can be difficult to understand. This is why the priest or deacon explains the meaning of the readings to us in a homily. The homily also tells us how to live God's word in our own lives.

PROFESSION OF FAITH STAND

We Profess Our Faith

Having heard God's word in the readings and having heard an explanation of those readings in the homily, we now want to proclaim before everyone that we believe. We believe what God has told us; we believe that he has called us; we believe that he loves us. To say all of this, we profess our faith with the creed.

THE NICENE CREED

WE believe in one God,
    the FATHER, THE ALMIGHTY,
maker of heaven and earth,
of all that is seen and unseen.

We believe in one Lord, JESUS CHRIST,
the only Son of God,
eternally begotten of the Father,
God from God, Light from Light,
true God from true God,
begotten, not made, one in Being with the Father

Through him all things were made.
For us men and for our salvation
    he came down from heaven:

All bow at the following words up to: and became man.

by the power of the Holy Spirit
    he was born of the Virgin Mary, and became man.

For our sake he was crucified under Pontius Pilate;
    he suffered, died, and was buried.
    On the third day he rose again
        in fulfillment of the Scriptures;
    he ascended into heaven
        and is seated at the right hand of the Father.

He will come again in glory to judge the living and the
dead,
and his kingdom will have no end.

We believe in the HOLY SPIRIT, the Lord, the giver of life,
who proceeds from the Father and the Son.
With the Father and the Son he is worshiped and
glorified.
He has spoken throught the Prophets.
We believe in one holy catholic and apostolic Church.
We acknowledge one baptism for the forgiveness of
sins.
We look for the resurrection of the dead,
and the life of the world to come. Amen.

—————— OR   THE APOSTLES' CREED ——————

I BELIEVE in God, the Father almighty,
creator of heaven and earth.

I believe in Jesus Christ, his only Son, our Lord.
He was conceived by the power of the Holy Spirit
and born of the Virgin Mary.
He suffered under Pontius Pilate,
was crucified, died, and was buried.
He descended to the dead.
On the third day he rose again.
He ascended into heaven,
and is seated at the right hand of the Father.
He will come again to judge the living and the dead.

I believe in the Holy Spirit,
the holy catholic Church,
the communion of saints,
the forgiveness of sins,
the resurrection of the body,
and the life everlasting. Amen.

GENERAL INTERCESSIONS

We Pray for Our Brothers and Sisters in Christ

We then close the first part of the Mass by saying the General Intercessions, also known as the Prayer of the Faithful. When we go to Mass, we pray not only for ourselves but also for all who need God's help.

The priest usually begins and ends the General Intercessions and someone else reads the intentions for which we are praying. We add our voices to this prayer by repeating the response that has been chosen. Very often, our response is:

People: Lord, hear our prayer.

We begin by praying for the Church. We pray for the Pope, the bishops, priests, all deacons, and all of the people of God. We pray that we might all answer God's call in a loving manner.

We pray for public authorities, the leaders of our nation, and all the people of the world.

We also pray for those who have a special need. We pray for the poor, for those who are sick, for those who are sad, and for anyone else who might need our prayers.

We pray for those who have died. We remember them because we want to share our love with them and pray that they might be with God in heaven.

Finally, we pray for our own local community and our particular needs.

The Prayer of the Faithful closes the first part of the Mass, which is called the Liturgy of the Word.

LITURGY OF THE EUCHARIST

SIT

PREPARATION SONG — *While the gifts of the people are brought forward to the priest and are placed on the altar, a song is sung. The gifts are bread and wine and whatever else we offer for the needs of the Church and for the poor.*

15

PREPARATION OF THE GIFTS

We Place the Bread on the Altar

The priest takes the bread and says in a quiet voice:

Blessed are you, Lord, God of all creation.
Through your goodness we have this bread to offer,
which earth has given and human hands have made.
It will become for us the bread of life.

If there is no singing, we may respond.

Blessed be God for ever.

We Place the Wine on the Altar

He then takes the wine and says in a quiet voice:

Blessed are you, Lord, God of all creation.
Through your goodness we have this wine to offer,
fruit of the vine and work of human hands.
It will become our spiritual drink.

If there is no singing, we may respond.

Blessed be God for ever.

*The priest washes his hands, asking God to wash away his sins.
He then says,*

INVITATION TO PRAYER   STAND

We ask God to Accept Our Sacrifice

Priest: Pray, brethren, that our sacrifice
may be acceptable to God, the almighty Father.

People: **May the Lord accept the sacrifice at your
hands
for the praise and glory of his name,
for our good, and the good of all his Church.**

PRAYER OVER THE GIFTS

We pray for God's Grace

*When we have offered our gifts, the priest says the Prayer over
the Gifts. Like the Opening Prayer, there is a special one for each
day of the year.*

At the end:

People: **Amen.**

EUCHARISTIC PRAYER

The priest now begins the Eucharistic Prayer. This is the prayer that will change the bread and wine into the body and blood of our Lord.

Priest: The Lord be with you.

People: And also with you.

Priest: Lift up your hearts.

People: We lift them up to the Lord.

Priest: Let us give thanks to the Lord our God.

People: It is right to give him thanks and praise.

The priest then calls upon the Lord with a prayer called the Preface. We respond to that prayer by singing or saying the same prayer that the angels sing before God's throne:

HOLY, HOLY, HOLY

We Praise God in Union with the Angels

Priest and People:

**Holy, Holy, Holy Lord, God of power and might,
heaven and earth are full of your glory.
Hosanna in the highest.
Blessed is he who comes in the name of the Lord.
Hosanna in the highest.**

18

HOLY, HOLY, HOLY — *The priest and people unite with all the angels to praise God the Father and Jesus whom he has sent.* **19**

THE BREAD BECOMES THE BODY OF CHRIST — *The priest recalls Jesus' words at the Last Supper and by God's power the bread becomes the body of Christ.*

WORDS OF INSTITUTION

The Bread and Wine Becomes Christ's Body and Blood

There are a number of different Eucharistic Prayers that the priest can use, but they all use the words that Jesus said over the bread and wine. The priest takes the bread and says,

Before he was given up to death,
a death he freely accepted,
he took bread and gave you thanks.
He broke the bread,
gave it to his disciples, and said:

"Take this, all of you, and eat it:
this is my body which will be given up for you."

The priest holds up the body of Christ for all the people to see.

The priest then takes the cup filled with the wine and says,

When supper was ended, he took the cup.
Again he gave you thanks and praise,
gave the cup to his disciples and said:

"Take this, all of you, and drink from it:
this is the cup of my blood,
the blood of the new and everlasting covenant.
It will be shed for you and for all
so that sins may be forgiven.
Do this in memory of me."

The priest holds up the cup that contains the blood of Christ for all the people to see.

THE WINE BECOMES THE BLOOD OF CHRIST — *The priest recalls Jesus' words at the Last Supper and by God's power the wine becomes the blood of Christ.*

MEMORIAL ACCLAMATION

We Proclaim the Mystery of Our Faith

We are so happy that God is giving us this very special gift that we feel like crying out for joy. The priest invites us to do this in the Memorial Acclamation. This prayer is a short profession of faith. There are four different ones that we can use:

Priest: Let us proclaim the mystery of faith.

People:

A   **Christ has died,
Christ is risen,
Christ will come again.**

———————— OR ————————

B   **Dying you destroyed our death,
rising you restored our life,
Lord Jesus, come in glory.**

———————— OR ————————

C   **When we eat this bread and drink this cup,
we proclaim your death, Lord Jesus,
until you come in glory.**

———————— OR ————————

D   **Lord, by your cross and resurrection
you have set us free.
You are the Savior of the world.**

GREAT AMEN

We Give Our Assent to All That Has Taken Place

At the end of the Eucharistic Prayer, we join the priest in giving glory to the Father through Jesus:

Through him,
  with him,
in him,
in the unity of the Holy
  Spirit,
all glory and honor is
  yours,
almighty Father,
for ever and ever.
People: Amen.

COMMUNION RITE
LORD'S PRAYER

We Speak to God our Father in the Words
Jesus Taught Us

*After the Eucharistic Prayer is finished, we prepare to receive
Jesus in communion by saying the prayer that Jesus taught us. We
praise God, ask for our daily bread, and beg forgiveness for our
sins.*

Priest and People:

Our Father, who art in heaven,
    hallowed be thy name;
thy kingdom come;
thy will be done on earth as it is in
    heaven.
Give us this day our daily bread;
and forgive us our trespasses
as we forgive those who trespass
    against us;
and lead us not into temptation,
but deliver us from evil.

LORD'S PRAYER — *Our preparation for receiving Jesus in Holy Communion continues with the "Our Father," the prayer that Jesus taught us to say.*

Priest: Deliver us, Lord, from every evil,
and grant us peace in our day.
In your mercy keep us free from sin
and protect us from all anxiety
as we wait in joyful hope
for the coming of our Savior, Jesus Christ.

People: **For the kingdom, the power, and the
glory
are yours, now and for ever.**

SIGN OF PEACE

We Offer a Sign of Peace to Each Other

*Before we receive the body and blood of Jesus, we have to
make peace with each other.*

The priest says a prayer for peace and unity that ends with:

Priest: For ever and ever.

People: **Amen.**

Priest: The peace of the Lord be with you always.

People: **And also with you.**

Priest: Let us offer each other the sign of peace.

We give a sign of peace to those around us.

BREAKING OF THE BREAD

We Ask for Mercy and Peace

We then call upon Jesus to prepare us so that we might be ready to receive communion. We say,

People:

Lamb of God, you take away the sins of the
world:
have mercy on us.

Lamb of God, you take away the sins of the
world:

Lamb of God, you take away the sins of the
world:
grant us peace.

COMMUNION

We Ask God to Make Us Worthy
to Receive Communion

The priest invites us to receive Jesus our Savior who comes to us in communion. He prays with us, asking God to make us worthy to receive his great gift.

Priest and People:

Lord, I am not worthy to receive you,
but only say the word and I shall be healed.

He then receives communion.

It is very important that we remind ourselves of what we are about to do when we receive communion. We do not want to go up to receive it just because everyone else is going or just because we do it every Sunday. We should remind ourselves that this is the body and blood of our Lord. We should receive it because we want to be one with Jesus and we want to be like him.

COMMUNION — We receive the bread that has become the body (and blood) of our Lord. This is God's most special gift to us.

We Receive Jesus

We then go up to receive the body and blood of Jesus. The priest or the minister of the eucharist says:

Priest: The body of Christ.

Communicant: Amen.

Priest: The blood of Christ.

Communicant: Amen.

This response means that we really want to be one with God.

The Communion Song is sung while communion is given to the faithful.

PERIOD OF SILENCE OR SONG OF PRAISE `SIT`

We Praise God

After communion there may be a period of silence, or a song of praise may be sung.

PRAYER AFTER COMMUNION

We Ask for the Grace of Communion

Priest: Let us pray.

When everyone has finished receiving communion, the priest says a prayer called the Prayer after Communion. Like the Opening Prayer and the Prayer over the Gifts, it is different for each day of the year. The prayer usually asks that we might be able to live with our whole heart and our entire love the things that we have promised to do when we received communion.

At the end:

Priest: Through Christ our Lord.

People: Amen.

CONCLUDING RITE

The Mass closes with a sign of the cross, just as it began with one. This time the sign of the cross is a blessing.

BLESSING

We Receive God's Blessing from the Priest

Priest: The Lord be with you.

People: And also with you.

Priest: May almighty God bless you,
            the Father, and the Son, and the Holy Spirit.

People: Amen.

DISMISSAL

We Are Sent Out to Bring Christ to Others

Deacon (or priest):

A   Go in the peace of Christ.

———————— OR ————————

B   The Mass is ended, go in peace.

———————— OR ————————

C   Go in peace to love and serve the Lord.

People: Thanks be to God.

The Recessional Song ends our celebration.

As we go forth from the Church, we realize that we have been changed. We have received the body and blood of our Lord, and this has made us his apostles. We now go forth into the world to carry the love of Jesus to everyone whom we will meet.